DO IT YOURSELF

Changing States

Solids, Liquids, and Gases

Will Hurd

www.raintreepublishers.co.uk
Visit our website to find out more information about Raintree books.

To order:

☎ Phone 0845 6044371

🖹 Fax +44 (0) 1865 312263

🖥 Email myorders@capstonepub.co.uk

Customers from outside the UK please telephone +44 1865 312262

Raintree is an imprint of Capstone Global Library Limited, a company incorporated in England and Wales having its registered office at 7 Pilgrim Street, London, EC4V 6LB – Registered company number: 6695582

"Raintree" is a registered trademark of Pearson Education Limited, under licence to Capstone Global Library Limited

Edited by Louise Galpine and Rachel Howells
Designed by Richard Parker and Tinstar Design Ltd
Original illustrations © Capstone Global Library Ltd
Illustrations: Oxford Designers and Illustrators and Geoff Ward (p. 37)
Picture research by Hannah Taylor and Fiona Orbell
Production by Alison Parsons
Originated by Dot Gradations Ltd.
Printed in China by Leo Paper Products Ltd.

ISBN 978 0 4311 1319 7 (hardback)
13 12 11 10 09
10 9 8 7 6 5 4 3 2 1

ISBN 978 0 4311 1326 5 (paperback)
14 13 12 11 10
10 9 8 7 6 5 4 3 2 1

British Library Cataloguing in Publication Data
Hurd, Will
Changing states : solids, liquids, and gases. - (Do it yourself)
530.4
A full catalogue record for this book is available from the British Library.

Acknowledgements

We would like to thank the following for permission to reproduce photographs: © Alamy pp. **15** (Leigh Smith Images), **40** (Tom Uhlman); © Corbis pp. **19** (Alison Wright), **21** (Visuals Unlimited), **22** (So Hing-Keung), **27** (NASA/epa), **29** (Frans Lanting), **36** (Steven Vidler/Eurasia Press); © David Corby p. **39**; © Getty pp. **7** (Edgardo Contreras), **9** (Neo Vision), **30** (Nick Clements); © Hollandse Hoogte/eyevine p. **17** (Bas Beentjes); © Photolibrary pp. **5** (Liysa), **11** (Francis E. Caldwell), **14** (Jeffrey Hamilton), **33** (Scott W. Smith), **35** (Dani/Jeske); © Science Photo Library pp. **31** (Dirk Wiersma), **43** (NASA/ESA/ STSCI/ Hubble Heritage Team); © Still Pictures pp. **4** (McPhotos), **23** (Nigel Hicks/WWI), **34** (R. Gerth), **41** (Ingrid Visser/SplashdownDirect/Splashdown), **42** (A. Vossberg/VISUM).

Cover photograph of water streaming down onto stacked clear ice cubes, reproduced with permission of © TongRo (Beateworks/ Corbis).

We would like to thank Harold Pratt for his invaluable help in the preparation of this book.

Every effort has been made to contact copyright holders of material reproduced in this book. Any omissions will be rectified in subsequent printings if notice is given to the publishers.

Disclaimer

Contents

Any words appearing in the text in bold, **like this**, are explained in the glossary.

Matter is all around us

Imagine yourself on a camping trip with your family. Your tent is pitched near a lake, and a fresh, gentle breeze blows. You may not realize it, but everything around you is **matter**. Matter exists in three forms, or states – solid, liquid, and gas. Your tent is a solid, the water in the lake is a liquid, and the air around you is made up of gases.

Matter is anything in the entire universe that takes up space and has **mass**. The amount of space an object occupies is the object's **volume**. For example, a golf ball and a ping-pong ball are about the same size. They take up about the same amount of space, so they have about the same volume. Mass is a measure of how much matter is in something. Even though the golf ball and the ping-pong ball have about the same volume, the golf ball is heavier. There is more matter in a golf ball. A golf ball's mass is greater than that of a ping-pong ball.

Everything on Earth is made of matter, whether it is natural or made by humans.

What is matter made of?

All matter is made up of **atoms**. Atoms are the basic building blocks of matter. There are more than 100 different types of atoms, and each kind of atom is an **element**. Iron, carbon, oxygen, and hydrogen are examples of elements.

Atoms of the elements oxygen and hydrogen can combine to make water. When atoms combine to make a new substance, they create **molecules**. An atom or a molecule is the smallest particle of a substance that is still considered to be that substance. For example, if you separate one molecule of water from a puddle, that molecule is still water. It is a combination of two atoms of hydrogen and one atom of oxygen (H_2O). But if you separate the atoms, you do not have water any more – just hydrogen and oxygen. A single atom of hydrogen is the smallest particle of hydrogen that is considered to be hydrogen. The same is true of oxygen.

About the experiments

Carrying out the experiments in this book will help you to investigate matter for yourself. The experiments use simple, everyday materials and tools. Always read through the instructions before you start, and take your time. You will need an adult to help with some of the experiments.

5

Molecules and states of matter

Steps to follow

1 Completely fill the jar with marbles and screw on the lid. Shake the jar up and down and side to side. What do you observe?

2 Unscrew the lid and pour out half of the marbles. Put the lid back on and, with one hand, move the jar all around – sideways, upside-down, around in circles. How do the marbles move? Is there space between them as they move?

3 Unscrew the lid again. This time remove all but four marbles from the jar. Shake the jar up and down quickly. Now what do the marbles do?

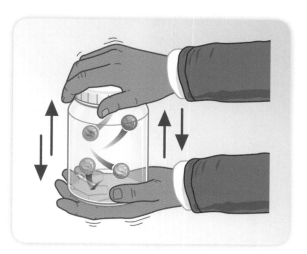

What do molecules do?

Molecules and **atoms** are always in motion. Think about the marbles in the jar in step one of the experiment. The closely packed marbles in the full jar are still able to move – but only a little. This is like the molecules in a solid. They don't do much more than vibrate, as they are usually arranged in a fixed, regular pattern.

The marbles in the jar in step 2 of the experiment had more room to move around. When you moved the jar around in circles, the marbles swirled like a drink in a glass. This shows how the molecules in a liquid are arranged. The molecules are quite close together, but less so than in a solid. They are free to move around and pass one another, and they have no fixed pattern.

Step 3 of the experiment, with only four marbles in the jar, shows how the molecules in a gas are arranged. There is plenty of room between the molecules, much more so than in a solid or a liquid. The molecules in a gas are free to move around in whatever direction they can.

The molecules in a cake cannot move much, but the molecules in a balloon can cause it to float up out of your reach!

Molecules on the move

For this activity you will need:

* a glass of very cold (refrigerated) water
* a glass of warm water
* a glass of very hot (but not **boiling**) water
* blue, green, and red food colouring
* two helpers.

1 Line the glasses up with a small space between them.

2 Quickly, before the water temperatures have a chance to change, you and each of your helpers put two drops of the food colourings in each glass – blue in cold, green in warm, red in hot.

3 In which glass does the colouring spread quickest, until all of the water is coloured?

What is smell?

When you smell something, your nose is actually interacting with molecules of that thing. For example, when garlic is frying in a pan, the heat helps to free molecules of the garlic. They then float through the air until they enter your nose. Special sensors send the "garlic" signal to your brain, which causes you to smell garlic.

Molecules are always moving

Whatever a substance's state of **matter**, its molecules or atoms are in motion. As you already know, the molecules or atoms in a solid move just a little. The molecules or atoms in a liquid move more freely, and the molecules in a gas can bounce and ping wherever.

The movement of the food colouring through the water is made possible by the movement of the water molecules. The speed at which the red food colouring moved, as opposed to the green and especially the blue, shows that applying heat to substances makes their molecules move faster. The hot water spread the food colouring the fastest of all.

Solids

Steps to follow

Make a solid

For this activity you will need:
* plaster of Paris
* water
* a 350-ml (12-fl. oz) disposable plastic cup
* a 475-ml (16-fl. oz) plastic cup
* a soup bowl.

1 Ask an adult to help you make 350 ml (12 fl. oz) of plaster of Paris in the cup.

2 After the plaster hardens, take it out of the cup. This is your 350-ml (12 fl. oz) plaster cast. Hint: If the plaster is stuck in the cup, you can cut the cup away with scissors.

4 Now put the cast in the bowl. Again, what do you observe? How does the cast behave when the shape of the container changes?

3 Put your plaster cast in the 475-ml (16-fl. oz) cup and make some observations. Does the shape of the cast change when its container changes?

⚠ **Warning**: Adult help will be needed for this experiment.

You can count on a solid

There is a reason why people say a reliable person is "as solid as a rock". Solids, by their nature, do not change easily. The plaster cast is a typical solid. And, like every solid, it has a definite **volume** and a definite shape. As you saw, putting a solid in a different container did not change its shape at all. This is true because the **molecules** in a solid are packed together closely, and attractive forces hold them together.

It takes work to change the shape of a solid. For example, think about a tree. Can its shape be changed easily? What do people do to change the shapes of trees? A saw can be used to cut the tree down and into pieces. But it takes energy – the power of a person's arms or a chainsaw's engine – to do it. When the energy is applied, and the tree's shape is changed, each new solid piece has its own shape.

A logger uses a saw to change the shape of this solid (a tree).

Steps to follow

1 Pour the hot water into the jar. It is important to keep the water warm throughout the process. Carefully warm it in the microwave for 15–30 seconds when you feel it get too cool.

2 Begin adding the salt one teaspoonful at a time. Stir until the salt dissolves after each teaspoonful you add. Stop adding salt when the last teaspoonful will not dissolve.

Growing crystals

For this activity you will need:

* 235 ml (8 fl. oz) of hot tap water
* red food colouring
* a 350-ml (12-fl. oz) jar
* 500 g (18 oz) of table salt
* a teaspoon
* a stirring rod or spoon
* a pencil
* a paper clip
* a 15-cm (6-in) piece of dental floss
* a microwave oven
* a magnifying glass.

3 Add a few drops of food colouring to the solution and stir.

4 Tie one end of the dental floss to the paper clip. Tie the other end around the middle of the pencil.

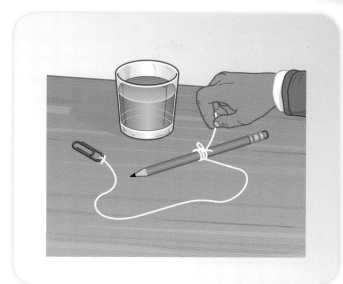

 5 Rest the pencil across the mouth of the jar, with the paper clip dangling in the saltwater solution. The paper clip should hang down nearly to the bottom of the jar, but should not touch it.

 6 Wait 24 hours before you look to see what is happening. Use a magnifying glass to get a close look at your results.

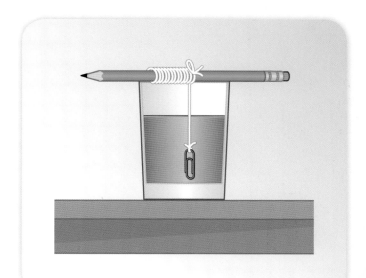

 7 Let the experiment continue for several days and see how your results change.

A solid crystal structure

What you see growing on the paper clip is a crystal of the **mineral** halite, or rock salt. You can see these crystals, but deep inside halite and most other solids are other crystals you cannot see. The **atoms** in these solids are not only close together – they are grouped into regular, repeating shapes. This is a **crystal structure**. A molecule's crystal structure determines how each solid looks, feels, and behaves.

The minerals diamond and graphite show what this means. Both are made up of only the **element** carbon. If they are both just carbon, why aren't they the same? Diamond and graphite form in very different ways. Their atoms come together differently, and they have very different crystal structures. Diamonds are shiny and come in many colours. Also, diamond is the hardest natural thing on Earth. Some diamonds are used to saw and drill through tough rocks. Graphite, on the other hand, is extremely soft and slippery. It is so soft that it is used as the "lead" in pencils. It has a dull appearance and a dark grey colour.

A piece of graphite and a diamond are both made up of only one element – carbon. But they look so different!

A world of different solids

It would be impossible to imagine all of the different combinations of appearance, shape, and feel of Earth's solids.

One solid, the rock marble, can be any of a number of colours – white, grey, black, or even red. It is a fairly soft rock that does not shatter when struck. So, artists through the ages, such as Leonardo da Vinci and Michelangelo, have used marble to make sculptures. Today, papers, paints, and plastics are made stronger by adding finely ground white marble to them.

Another solid, glass, is clear, stiff, and breaks easily. You know all about the type of glass that is used in windows and bottles, but other types of glass occur naturally. Obsidian is a natural glass that forms when a certain type of lava cools and hardens. Ancient peoples worked out they could make very sharp knives and arrowheads from obsidian if it was split in just the right way. Obsidian is still used today. For example, obsidian surgical knives are much sharper than steel ones.

Liquids

Pouring liquids

For this activity you will need:

* 350 ml (12 fl. oz) of water in a glass

* a flower vase

* a bowl.

Note: Both the vase and the bowl should be able to hold at least 350 ml (12 fl. oz).

1 Pour the water from the glass into the vase. What do you see? Is the shape of the water any different now than it was in the glass?

2 Now pour the water from the vase into the bowl. What do you see now? Did the water's shape change or stay the same?

Liquids go with the flow

Liquids are like solids in that they have a definite **volume**. In other words, a liquid takes up a measurable amount of space. When you need one litre (two pints) of water for a recipe, you can easily measure it out.

As you saw in the experiment, a liquid changes its shape easily. A liquid in an oval container has an oval shape. A liquid in a square container has a square shape. As you learned earlier, the **molecules** in a liquid are quite close together, but they are not attached and ordered in the same way as a solid's molecules. The molecules move freely, and liquids are able to flow.

Controlling the flow

People often want to control the flow of liquids for important reasons. In the Netherlands, a system of solid barriers, called dykes, keep the waters of the North Sea from flooding large areas of the low-lying country.

Solid barriers can keep ocean waters from flowing over land.

Oil and water

For this activity you will need:

* 125 ml (4.4 fl. oz) of water dyed with red food colouring
* 125 ml (4.4 fl. oz) of water dyed with blue food colouring
* 125 ml (4.4 fl. oz) of water dyed with green food colouring
* 125 ml (4.4 fl. oz) of yellow-coloured cooking oil (sunflower oil or peanut oil will work)
* two empty 250-ml (8.8-fl. oz) glass measuring jugs.

1 Pour the red and blue water together into one of the empty measuring jugs. What do you observe?

2 Now pour the green water into the other empty measuring jug.

3 Slowly pour the oil into the green water in that jug. What do you see? Is the behaviour of these two liquids different from that of the red and blue water? How is it different?

Dense waters

Salt water is more dense than fresh water, so when you swim in the salty ocean you float higher in the water. The extremely salty waters of the Dead Sea, on the border of Israel and Jordan, are very dense. People swimming in the Dead Sea for the first time are often shocked. The water's density makes them feel like they are laying on the water's surface!

Getting the pages of a newspaper wet is not a problem when you can float as high as this! The Dead Sea has a salt content almost seven times that of the ocean.

Some things just don't mix

Unfortunately, tankers that transport oil on the oceans sometimes have accidents and spill oil. But oil does not mix in with the water. It forms a film on the water. Why does oil float on water? In the experiment, the green water and the oil were of equal volume, 125 ml (4.4 fl. oz). But there is less **mass** in 125 ml (4.4 fl. oz) of oil than there is in 125 ml (4.4 fl. oz) of water. When two things have equal volumes but one has less mass than the other, it is said to be less **dense**. This is true of solids, liquids, and even gases. In the example of the golf ball and the ping-pong ball given on page 4, which ball has the greater density? The golf ball has greater density, because it has greater mass in an equal amount of volume.

Surface tension

For this activity you will need:

* a small sewing needle
* a sheet of toilet paper
* a deep bowl that is wider than the toilet paper
* water.

1 Fill the bowl about three-quarters full of water.

2 Place the needle on the centre of the toilet paper.

3 Gently place the toilet paper on top of the water. What happens when the toilet paper sinks?

(If the needle does not float, get a new piece of toilet paper, dry the needle, and try again. It can be a little tricky!)

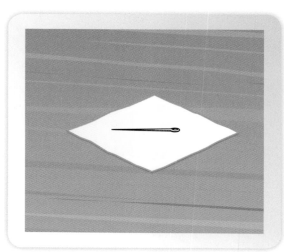

How does it work?

In liquids, molecules experience a weak attractive force that can draw them together. Picture one molecule of water deep inside the bowl of water in the experiment. It is surrounded on all sides by other water molecules. This molecule shares its attractive force equally with all of the molecules above it, below it, and around it. Shared equally in this way, the force is very weak. But molecules at the surface have no molecules above them. So their attraction is shared mostly with other surface molecules. As a result, their attraction is stronger, and a "film" forms on the surface. This film, known as **surface tension**, is what supported the needle.

Pulling together

Surface tension explains why water forms into droplets. A falling drop of water is surrounded by air. The surface is all around it. The water molecules pull together on all sides and form the tightest shape possible, a sphere.

This pond skater is standing on the water because of surface tension.

Essential water

Every living thing on Earth relies on liquid water for its survival. A plant without water begins to wither and die quickly. Animals caught in droughts can only last a few days without a drink. People are much the same. Most people could not survive more than a week without water. The water we take in comes from anything we drink. Juice, milk, fizzy drinks – they are all drinks that begin with water. Most foods have some water in them, too.

Water's uses

People use water for many things other than drinking. Boats that transport goods and people all over the world float on oceans, lakes, and rivers. Dams built on rushing rivers turn the energy of the water's movement into **electricity**. People use water to keep themselves and their homes clean. They also use water for recreation – swimming, surfing, water skiing, and other fun activities.

The water in Hong Kong's Victoria Harbour allows this ferry to take people where they want to go.

The dangers of water

Sometimes water can have harmful effects on people and other things. The movement of water can cause **erosion**. Erosion strips away valuable lands, such as farm and forest soils, and often does its damage over time. **Tsunamis** (pronounced soo·NAHM·eez), on the other hand, can cause a catastrophe in the blink of an eye. A tsunami is a series of waves in the ocean caused by a natural event such as an underwater earthquake or a landslide. When these waves crash into coastal areas and islands where people live, they can destroy property and threaten many lives.

A tsunami is terrible but it is a natural event that cannot be prevented. Polluted water, however, comes from human actions. **Pesticides** washed off of farms, waste from factories, and many other pollutants foul Earth's waters. Water **pollution** is a threat to human health, but it also threatens plant and animal life worldwide. For example, in 2007, the baiji, a freshwater dolphin that lived only in the Yangtze River in China, was declared **extinct**. This means that it no longer exists as a **species**. Water pollution from factories was a major contributor to the baiji's fate.

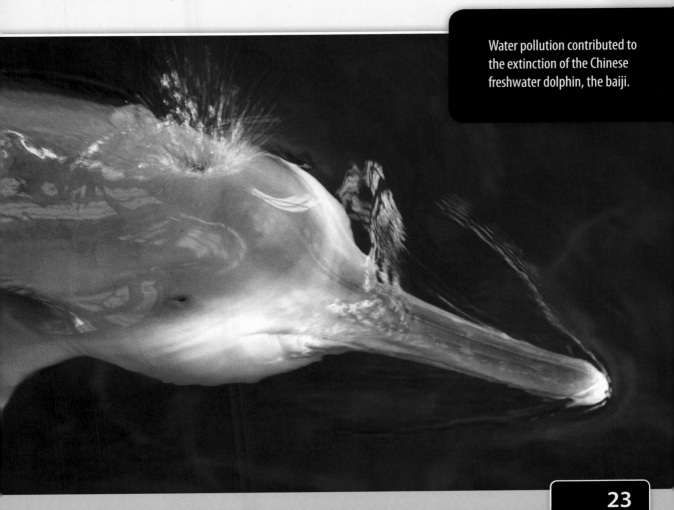

Water pollution contributed to the extinction of the Chinese freshwater dolphin, the baiji.

Gases

Does gas have mass?

For this activity you will need:

* two plastic rubbish bags with twist ties
* a metre stick (yardstick)
* some string.

1 Take the end of the string and tie it around the exact centre of the metre stick (yardstick).

2 Get an adult to help you secure the other end to the ceiling, so that the stick is about 1.5 metres (5 feet) above the floor. The best way would be to pin the string to the ceiling, but tying it to an overhead beam or a hook will work, too.

3 Squeeze all the air out of the bags and put the twist ties around the openings. Tie one bag to each end of the stick. Do they balance? They should.

4 Now untie one of the bags, fill it with air, and put the twist tie back on tightly. Tie it back to the stick. Do the two bags still balance?

 Warning: Adult help will be needed for this experiment.

Gases are not empty space

With your simple scale, you should have seen that the bag filled with air weighed more than the empty bag. This shows that air, which is a mixture of gases, has **mass**. The demonstration on page 6 showed that gases contain **molecules**, so it follows that they have mass, too.

Like a liquid, a gas has no definite shape, but what about a gas's **volume**? Neither a solid nor a liquid changes volume easily – does a gas? What do you think would happen if a litre (2 pints) of oxygen were pumped into an empty 2-litre (4-pint) container? The gas would expand, or spread out, to fill the entire container. Its volume begins as 1 litre (2 pints) but expands to 2 litres (4 pints).

Visualize this by imagining six people crowded into a lift. Each person represents a gas molecule. When the lift gets to the bottom floor, the people get out and walk into the lobby – a much larger space. They spread out and move around, and the space they are in is larger, but there are still only six of them.

People who spread out after leaving a packed lift behave very much like gases.

What is air?

The air-filled space that surrounds the Earth is called the **atmosphere**. The air that fills Earth's atmosphere is a mixture of many gases, but it is mostly nitrogen (78 percent) and oxygen (21 percent). Tiny amounts of other gases — carbon dioxide, water vapour, hydrogen, and others — make up the remaining one percent.

The amounts of the gases that make up air have been about the same for a long time. Our planet uses, moves, and recycles **elements** and gases very well. For example, animals such as deer take in oxygen, but give off carbon dioxide and water vapour. When living things, such as logs, die and rot, they too give off carbon dioxide. Living plants take in carbon dioxide and give off oxygen and water vapour. Unfortunately, human activities are changing the levels of gases in the atmosphere. Carbon dioxide levels are rising, a situation that is proving disastrous for the planet.

Plants and animals help keep several elements going through Earth's atmosphere.

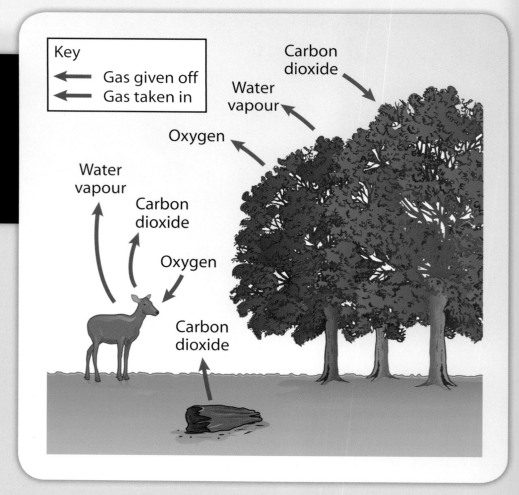

Key

← Gas given off
← Gas taken in

Strong winds

Winds blow across our planet as a natural result of the heat of the sun acting on the atmosphere. Sometimes these winds cause problems. For example, a tornado is a violent, rotating wind that moves along the Earth's surface. The winds in a tornado can move at up to 480 kilometres (300 miles) per hour. Tornadoes can wipe out entire towns, causing great loss of life and property damage.

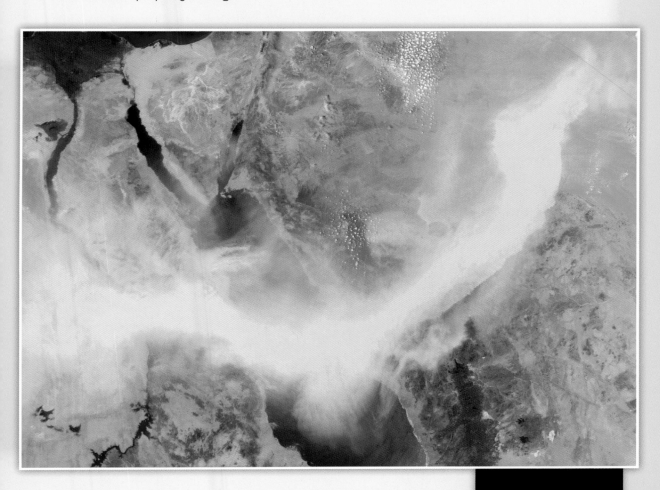

Strong winds that cause huge sandstorms in northern Africa have had an unexpected, negative effect far away. The sands blow all the way across the Atlantic Ocean and come to rest in the Caribbean Sea. Scientists believe that a **fungus** that lives in the sands may be killing parts of Caribbean sealife. Also, the settling African sands have caused air **pollution** warnings as far away as Puerto Rico!

A satellite captures an image of a dust storm moving across northern Africa.

Physical changes: freezing and melting

Steps to follow

1 Fill the bowl halfway with water from the tap.

2 Put the bowl in the freezer and leave it for 4 hours. Take the bowl out of the freezer. What has happened to the water?

3 Remove what's in the bowl, put it in the saucepan, and put the pan on the hob. With an adult's help, turn the heat on low beneath the pan for 5 minutes only.

4 Let the pan stand for another 15 minutes. Describe what you see in the pan.

Note: Save the contents of your pan for the next experiment.

Warning: Adult help will be needed for this experiment.

Changing states

As you have learned so far, **matter** may exist in one of three different forms, or states: solid, liquid, or gas. But did you know that matter can change from one state to another? You have just seen matter change states, and this is known as a **physical change**. This means that although the look and feel of the water changed, it stayed water the whole time.

Think back to pages 6 and 7. There we saw, in a very simple way, how **molecules** are arranged in the three different states. When a liquid changes to a solid, the liquid's molecules, which are less tightly bound to one another, lose energy, slow down, and become more tightly bound. At that point a solid is formed.

Does this mean that a solid is more **dense** than a liquid? If so, why does ice float in water? In our experiment with oil and water, the less dense substance floated. The bonds of hydrogen and oxygen that make up water are special. That is why it is the only substance normally found as a solid, a liquid, and a gas at Earth's surface. For almost every other substance, however, its solid form is denser than its liquid form.

The sun's warmth causes a physical change in these icicles.

Changing from a liquid to a solid state

When something freezes, it changes from a liquid state to a solid state. This happens because as a liquid's temperature gets lower, its molecules lose energy and slow down. Finally, the molecules slow down so much that their attractive force holds them together, and a solid is formed. Think back to the marble experiment on page 6 to help you visualize how the molecules slow. The temperature at which this begins to happen is called the **freezing point**.

You are familiar with the liquid and solid forms of water. Water has to be cooled below room temperature to freeze, but what about other solids? Is a solid silver coin sitting on a table "frozen"? Yes, it is. Remember, anything that is solid is frozen. Water freezes at a temperature we consider to be cold: 0 °C (−32 °F). But silver freezes at a much higher temperature: 961 °C (1,763 °F)! Since the normal room temperature of 21 °C (70 °F) is far below that, the silver coin is frozen.

Is this bike frozen? Bike frames and wheels are solids, so yes, it is.

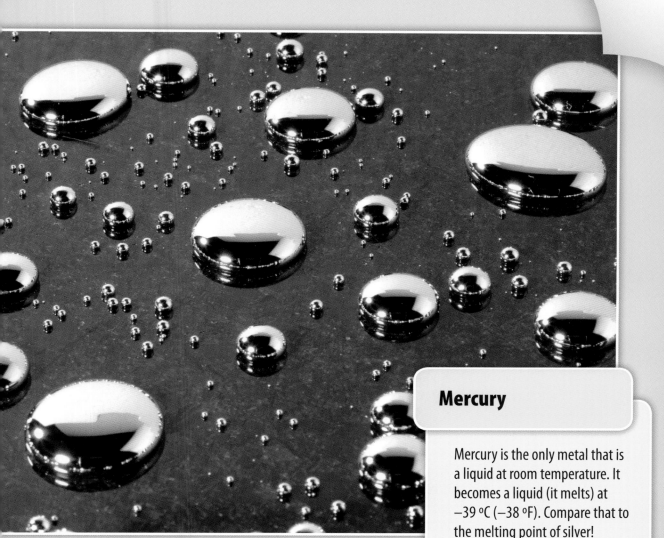

Mercury

Mercury is the only metal that is a liquid at room temperature. It becomes a liquid (it melts) at −39 ºC (−38 ºF). Compare that to the melting point of silver!

Changing from a solid to a liquid state

When something melts, it changes from a solid state to a liquid state. To see how things melt, turn the freezing process around. A solid's molecules are close together and linked, but they still move a little — almost shaking in place. When the temperature is raised, the molecules gain energy and then break free of one another. When the molecules can move past and around each other freely, the solid has become a liquid. The temperature where this begins to happen is called the **melting point**.

Note that a substance's melting and freezing points are exactly the same. Again, water is a good example. At 0 ºC (−32 ºF) water is ice. Any tiny fraction of a degree higher than that, and the ice begins to melt. So, the melting point of silver is also said to be 961 ºC (1,763 ºF). At any higher temperature the silver melts.

Physical changes: evaporation, boiling, and condensation

Steps to follow

1 Put the pan of water from the last experiment on the hob. Ask your adult helper to turn the heat beneath the pan to high. After 10 minutes or so, what happens?

2 Fill the mixing bowl halfway with ice, then cover the ice with cold water.

3 When the water in the pan is **boiling** and there is a lot of steam rising from the pan, ask your adult helper to put on the oven gloves and hold the bowl of ice water a few centimetres above the steaming pan. Get a close look. Is anything forming on the bottom of the bowl?

⚠️ **Warning**: Adult help will be needed for this experiment.

From water to water vapour, and back again

For this activity you will need:

* the pan of water from the last experiment (page 28)
* a metal mixing bowl
* some ice
* some water
* oven gloves

Changing states

When a liquid changes into a gas or a gas changes into a liquid, it goes through a **physical change**. As with the change from liquid to solid (or solid to liquid) the change involves the motion of and space between **molecules**. But the actual substance itself remains the same. In the experiment, while the state of the water changed, it was always water.

But why did the water vapour change into a liquid? For the same reason a glass of cold lemonade "sweats" on a hot day: **condensation**. Air always has some water vapour in it, especially close to the Earth's surface. Hot air can hold more water vapour than cold air, so a hot day has a good chance of being humid. The chilled glass makes the air that immediately surrounds it much colder than the air in general. The vapour in the air slows down and becomes water on the glass. You will learn more about condensation on page 35.

Condensation from warm air settles on a cold glass of lemonade.

Evaporation

Liquids can become gases either by evaporating or boiling. Although the same thing happens in the end, the two are different. **Evaporation** happens at the surface of a liquid. It can happen at many different temperatures. (This is an important difference from boiling.) Within any liquid, the molecules move and bounce around at different speeds. Sometimes a molecule moves fast enough to skip past the surface of the liquid and into the air. This molecule has evaporated – changed from a liquid to a gas.

Shrinking puddles

You've probably seen a puddle on the pavement near your home or school. As you walk past it at different times, you might notice it is shrinking. On a hot, sunny day it shrinks even faster. Even though the hot temperature did not make the water in the puddle boil, heat did make the water molecules move a little faster. Even more were able to break past the surface and float away.

The water in this puddle will become a gas through the slow process of evaporation.

Boiling

Boiling also changes a liquid to a gas. The difference between evaporation and boiling is that boiling produces bubbles. In the experiment on page 32, you should have seen the bubbles as the water boiled. These bubbles are pockets of vapour that quickly form below the water's surface. They rise to the top, burst, and release water vapour. Every liquid boils at a specific temperature, called its **boiling point**.

Bubbles of water vapour form in this boiling mud pool, rise, and then escape into the air.

Condensation

Gases change to liquids through condensation. Morning dew is a good example of condensation. After the sun goes down, the ground cools. As this happens, the air immediately above the ground cools, too. Water vapour molecules in the air begin to slow down as they cool, causing them to change from a gas to a liquid and settle on the grass.

Sublimation

Have you ever noticed old, shrunken ice cubes in your freezer? Sometimes a solid can turn into a gas, too. In this case, ice turns directly into water vapour without becoming liquid water first. This is called **sublimation**, and it works much like evaporation. Molecules are able to escape the solid's surface and become water vapour.

The water cycle

Water is different from all other **matter** on Earth. It is the only thing that is commonly found in nature in all three states: solid (ice), liquid (water), and gas (water vapour). It appears in all three states in the continual, natural process that uses and reuses water all over the world: the **water cycle**. A cycle is a series of events that happens over and over again. Think of a bicycle. As you ride, the wheels rotate again and again, repeating the same motion. Water can be thought of as moving in a circular motion through the Earth's systems, too.

Snow, lake water, and clouds show the three states of water in nature.

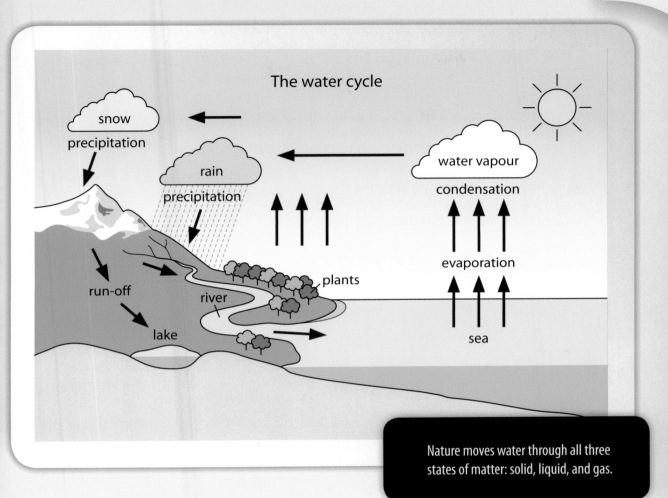

The water cycle

snow
precipitation

rain
precipitation

water vapour
condensation

run-off

river

plants

lake

evaporation

sea

Nature moves water through all three states of matter: solid, liquid, and gas.

How it works

There is no beginning or end to the water cycle, so let's just jump in where there is lots of water – the sea. Water in the sea evaporates constantly, turning into water vapour. The water vapour rises in the **atmosphere** and eventually clouds form through condensation. When clouds release their water as precipitation (which includes rain, hail, or snow) some becomes ice in snowcaps on mountains or in glaciers. Some water molecules in the ice undergo sublimation (turn directly into water vapour). But mostly, this ice melts and flows as liquid water run-off. Rainfall also nourishes plants, allowing them to grow. As we saw on page 26, these plants give off water as part of their growth. Rainfall and run-off end up in rivers and lakes. Water evaporates from rivers and lakes, just as it does from the sea. Rivers flow back into the sea where the water may evaporate and begin the cycle again.

Chemical changes

Steps to follow

Soda fizz

For this activity you will need:

* a 500-ml (17.6-fl.oz) glass bottle
* a balloon (give it a few stretches to loosen it up)
* a small funnel
* bicarbonate of soda
* white vinegar
* a tablespoon and measuring jug

1 Pull the open end of the balloon over the spout of the funnel. Using the funnel, put 2 tablespoons of bicarbonate of soda into the balloon.

2 Put 250 ml (8.8 fl. oz) of vinegar into the bottle.

3 Put the mouth of the balloon around the opening of the bottle. Let the rest of the balloon hang down so the bicarbonate of soda does not fall into the vinegar yet.

4 When you are ready, raise the balloon and let the bicarbonate of soda fall into the vinegar. What happens?

Changing substance

In your experiment, the balloon should have filled with a gas. This gas is carbon dioxide. Vinegar is a mild acid — a substance that can break down or dissolve some other substances. When it mixed with the bicarbonate of soda, something happened. A new substance, carbon dioxide, was formed. When a new substance is formed, a **chemical change** has taken place. By contrast, in a **physical change** the substance that is changing changes state, but the substance itself stays the same.

Rust changes the appearance of iron.

How can you tell a chemical change?

In the experiment, you witnessed one way to identify a chemical change — the production of bubbles. These are the type of bubbles that come from the interaction of different substances, not from heating something to its **boiling point**. A change in colour is another good sign that a chemical change is taking place. Rust is a perfect example. Over time, as iron is exposed to oxygen in the air, the two **elements** interact and a chemical change called oxidation takes place. The iron becomes weak and flaky, and the colour changes to the familiar orangey-brown colour of rust.

Burning

Throughout human history, people have relied on burning (also called **combustion**) to make their lives easier. Long ago, people burned wood to give them warmth or cook their food. Today, people mainly burn coal, oil, and gas to heat their homes. Power plants burn these three things to supply homes, schools, shops, and factories with **electricity**. Cars and lorries take people and goods all over the world, burning gasoline at the same time. Unfortunately, we have learned there is a price to pay for all of this burning. One major product of this common chemical change, combustion, is carbon dioxide. Human activities are raising the levels of carbon dioxide in the **atmosphere**, and it is getting a few degrees warmer in many parts of the planet.

Cars stack up on roads and motorways, releasing huge amounts of carbon dioxide into the atmosphere.

Global warming is melting the Arctic ice that polar bears need for survival.

Global warming

Carbon dioxide (CO_2) is one of several gases called **greenhouse gases**. Greenhouse gases get their name from the effect they have in the atmosphere. Just like the glass in a greenhouse where plants are grown, these gases trap heat beneath them and heat things up. Over the past 100 years, global temperatures have risen 0.6 °C (1.2 °F). This may not seem like much, but scientists say that this small change is already affecting nature. For example, since 1979 the amount of ice around the North Pole has shrunk at a rate of 7.7 percent per decade. This threatens animals living near the North Pole, such as the polar bear. In May 2008 the U.S. government listed the polar bear as a **species** in danger of **extinction**.

If people do not slow down or reverse their production of greenhouse gases soon, global temperatures will continue to rise. The future is uncertain, though, and scientists cannot be sure how much temperatures will rise. It is believed that they may increase anywhere from 1.4 °C–5.8 °C (2.2 °F–10 °F) by the year 2100. This could cause rising sea levels, stronger tropical storms, and animal and plant extinctions.

Beyond solids, liquids, and gases

It seems that when a fire is burning, it is difficult to stop staring at the flames. But did you ever ask yourself, what *are* flames? They are certainly not solid or liquid, and they are not a gas either. Flames actually belong to a fourth state of **matter** called **plasma**. Plasma is hard to understand, even for most adults. Even scientists only began to study it less than 100 years ago. The best way to think of plasma is that it is a gas that has an electrical charge. Other natural examples of matter that is plasma are the sun and lightning.

Plasma television images are produced when an electric charge turns a mixture of gases into plasma.

Who knows what other mysteries and discoveries await us in the outer limits of the universe?

What will the future bring?

Scientists have known about solids, liquids, and gases for many hundreds of years. But the recent discovery of plasma shows that science never stands still. The one thing that the history of science has shown is that nothing is final. Just within the last 75 years, scientists who study how the universe works have introduced the idea of "dark matter". It is called dark matter because no one can see it. But scientists know it is there because of how it affects things we can see, like stars and galaxies. Amazingly, scientists believe that this matter that we cannot see and know almost nothing about makes up most of the universe.

Dark matter is a fascinating mystery, but closer to home, scientists face many other tough challenges. **Pollution** and global warming stand out among them. The solids, liquids, and gases that make up our planet need help from all of Earth's residents, so keep learning and doing your part.

Glossary

atmosphere mixture of gases that surrounds the Earth

atom single particle of an element

boiling process by which a substance changes from a liquid to a gas

boiling point temperature at which a liquid changes to a gas through boiling

chemical change change in which one substance is converted into another. Oxidation is a chemical change that causes iron to turn to rust.

combustion chemical change that heats things up. An easier word for this is burning.

condensation process of changing from a gas to a liquid. Condensation on a window or mirror forms when water vapour in the air cools on the glass.

crystal structure unique arrangement of atoms or molecules in a solid. It is this arrangement that gives the substance its physical properties.

dense having a high mass per unit volume

electricity form of energy that we use to operate many devices and machines

element substance that cannot be broken down into simpler substances. An element is the basic building block of all matter.

erosion physical movement of weathered materials from one place to another

evaporation process of changing from a liquid to a gas without boiling

extinct when a species is extinct, it has died out and no longer exists

freezing point temperature at which a liquid changes to a solid

fungus (plural fungi) organism that causes plant disease and is often poisonous to humans. Mushrooms, toadstools, and moulds are all types of fungi.

greenhouse gas certain gases (but especially carbon dioxide) that are present in the atmosphere and reduce the loss of heat into space. The increase in greenhouse gases due to human activity is causing Earth's temperature to rise. This is called the greenhouse effect.

mass measurement of the amount of matter in an object

matter anything that exists as a solid, liquid, or gas

melting point temperature at which a solid changes to a liquid through melting

mineral solid substance found in nature

molecule smallest particle that a substance can be broken into while still keeping the properties of a substance

pesticide substance used to kill insects

physical change change in which a substance alters its state of matter but does not change into a new substance

plasma state of matter that can be thought of as an electrically charged gas

pollution act of damaging the environment through human-made waste

sextillion number so huge that it has 21 zeros. Six sextillion is written as 6,000,000,000,000,000,000,000.

species type of animals that are the same and can reproduce together

sublimation process by which a solid changes to a gas without becoming a liquid first

surface tension drawing together of the surface molecules in a liquid, which causes a film to form across the surface

tsunami massive sea wave produced by an underwater earthquake or other dramatic, natural event. The tsunami in Thailand in 2004 caused many people to lose their lives.

volume amount of space an object takes up

water cycle continuous movement of water from the Earth to the atmosphere and back to the Earth. Water appears naturally in its solid, liquid, and gas states in the water cycle.

Find out more

Books

Atoms and Molecules, Louise and Richard Spilsbury
(Heinemann Library, 2007)

Material Matters: States of Matter, Carol Baldwin
(Raintree, 2005)

The Science of Air: Projects and Experiments with Air and Flight, Steve Parker
(Heinemann Library, 2005)

Websites

Climate Change
www.bbc.co.uk/climate
This website provides a wide-ranging look at the topics of climate change, the **atmosphere**, weather, and what we can do to make a difference. A number of animations bring the site to life.

KS2 Bitesize
www.bbc.co.uk/schools/ks2bitesize/science/materials.shtml
BBC Bitesize provides online activities and information about materials.

Places to visit

Science Museum

Exhibition Road
South Kensington
London
SW7 2DD
Tel: 0870 870468

www.sciencemuseum.org.uk

Explore different materials and their uses in the Challenge of Materials Gallery. It is home to a wide range of fascinating objects, including a cardboard chair and a steel wedding dress.

Techniquest

Stuart Street
Cardiff Bay
Cardiff
CF10 5BW
Tel: 02920 475475

www.techniquest.org

This interactive museum includes a wide range of exhibits where you will find science in action. Launch a hot air balloon, watch a bubble race, or see a show about fire.

Index